"One of the chief challenges of adolescent religious education is to implement the disciples' request: Teach us to pray. *Teen Prayer Services* creatively grapples with this catechetical challenge, offering a solid blend of personal and communal prayer experiences. The themes focus on relevant adolescent concerns: friendship, forgiveness, freedom, happiness. Adolescents will be challenged to become daily pray-ers, critical Catholic thinkers, and disciples. High school catechists, religion teachers, and youth ministers will find these resources pastorally sensitive and relevant for teaching youth to pray."

Joseph P. Sinwell, D.Min.
Diocesan Director
of Religious Education
Diocese of Providence

"Kevin Regan's exciting new book, *Teen Prayer Services*, is down-to-earth, realistic, versatile, in touch with youth, and inspiring. It fills a real need for me as a high school catechist who is always looking for new ideas to lead my students in prayer. I am anxious to try several of the services with my own students.

Michael Pennock
Author, *Friendship in the Lord* (high school texts)

"Kevin Regan gets teens to pray in practical, down-to-earth ways. They are invited to meet their God within traditional and untraditional themes. Of particular note are the themes of God Our Mother, ecology, sexuality, reconciliation, failure, death, and decisions. Regan structures these prayer services in such a way that youth ministers and teens have to—and will want to—get involved as they move from sharing personal experiences to quiet time and response."

Dr. Greg Dues
Author, *Seasonal Prayer Services for Teenagers*

"Kevin Regan's *Teen Prayer Services* provokes thought and invites growth as teens look together at some pressing issues: the sensitivity of sexuality, their connectedness with Earth, the benefits of failure, and the hidden depths of love. Regan writes with compassionate understanding. He brings theology into present reality for young people; his prayer services challenge them to be a part of the world around them, to grow together in God's love."

Mobby Larson
Author, *Why Can't We Talk?* and *Prayers of a Christian Educator*

TEEN PRAYER SERVICES

20
Themes for Reflection

S. KEVIN REGAN

TWENTY-THIRD PUBLICATIONS
Mystic, Connecticut 06355

Third printing 1997

Twenty-Third Publications
P.O. Box 180
185 Willow Street
Mystic, CT 06355
(860) 536-2611
800-321-0411

ISBN: 0-89622-520-8
Library of Congress Catalog Card No. 92-81797

Dedication

To Kristen and Dan
for all the love and joy you bring into the world

Contents

	Introduction	1
1	Dragons and Demons: Overcoming Evil	3
2	Prejudice: A Different Way of Seeing	6
3	Friendship: God's Gift to Us	9
4	True Happiness: Being Myself	12
5	God: Our Holy Mother	16
6	Stewardwhip: Earth Is Our Mother	19
7	Peace: Discovering God's Way	23
8	Hide and Seek: God Invites Us to Freedom	26
9	Saying Thank You: The Meaning of Eucharist	29
10	Self-Esteem: Becoming the Hands of God	33
11	Sexuality: It's About Love	36
12	Forgiveness: A Light in the Darkness	40
13	Failure: A Time for Faith	43
14	Hope: In the Face of Death	46
15	Jonah and Jesus: Praying to Our Father	50
16	God Is With Us: In the Flesh	53
17	Choices: A Path to Freedom	56
18	Love: A Gift of the Heart	59
19	Suffering: A Way to Love	63
20	Prayer: Discipline for Disciples	66

TEEN PRAYER SERVICES

Introduction

Each of these prayer services in this book begin with an "Introduction" intended for the leader, which offers background information and helps the leader get a sense of the theme. The "Shared Experience" section offers time for adults and youth to share reflections and to reach common ground about the theme. It recognizes the fact that our shared experiences are "holy ground," the locus of God's activity. The "Getting Started" section points toward or introduces the Scripture to be used, and "Quiet Time" precedes the reading of Scripture. This is an essential aspect of these services since it invites the young to bring God's word to bear on the events that shape their lives. The "Response" gives participants the opportunity to take action by responding to God, highlighting the fact that God always takes the initiative and awaits our response. The "Conclusion" uses ritual and symbols to affirm the faith of the participants, and it celebrates Christian hope and solidarity.

These prayer services can be used in a variety of ways: to begin or end religion classes, as part of day-long or weekend retreat sessions, or as part of weekly or bi-weekly workshops or social gatherings. Religious education directors may also want to use them with parents and students in confirmation preparation sessions. Whatever the use, the goal is the same: to put our young people in touch with God through prayer.

When we pray with young people, we invite them to enter more conscientiously into this world, guided by the light of faith. John Shea has written that faith is interpreting the inescapable. This is one way of understanding the importance of prayer for the young. Prayer offers them and us a way of entering into the inner and outer complexities of life.

When we pray we open our hearts to God. Because the heart is understood as the deepest center of the person, what we do with the young is risky business, an act of becoming vulnerable.

This book is meant to help the young to touch life in all its paradoxes. It does not seek to convince them of anything nor to get anything from them. Rather it invites them into a dialogue begun in history, confirmed by tradition, and offered to them today ever new in Christ.

This way of prayer seeks to break the shell of indifference that society today has built around life's mysteries. It does not ask God to be present in our young people, for God already walks with them. Rather it invites them and us to remove the blinders that prevent us from seeing the truth. It invites God into their hearts and our hearts that we might move back to the way of love after we have missed the mark through sin.

This book is offered by a pilgrim on the journey, a pilgrim who is walking with the young through a time in their lives that is full of tribulation and joy, through an age that is so temporary yet so formative. I hope to offer these young people words of hope and healing. As Thomas Merton once wrote, what people need most today are words of healing, words that will help them overcome evil with good. This is my goal for these prayer services: to help young pray-ers overcome evil with good, to offer them words of hope and healing.

1

Dragons and Demons:
Overcoming Evil

Times for Use

Feast of Michael the Archangel (September 29), Martin Luther King Day (mid-January), and any occasion on which the issues of hunger, homelessness, alcohol or drug abuse are being discussed.

Materials Needed

Pictures of dragons, markers, crayons, or paints, index cards, pens or pencils.

Introduction

Ancient myths depict dragons as evil. Today, though we no longer fear dragons, we are not free from the evils earlier societies associated with them. Evil and tragedy still surround us.

In the United States alone, close to three million people are homeless. According to the bishops' Pastoral Letter on the Economy, one in every four American children under the age of six lives in poverty. More than one-third of all households headed by females are poor.

One-fifth of our world's population live in conditions of absolute poverty, and thousands of children die daily. Poverty, drug addiction, alcohol abuse, and domestic violence, especially to women, are all evils that we can't ignore. Our young people live in an environment that is demonic and idolatrous.

Yet, our world is also the sphere of the holy, the locus of God's continual saving action in history through Jesus. Our role is to help our teenagers turn to God for the strength to overcome evil with good. For this we must pray often, and this is the theme of this service.

Shared Experience

If you can locate a large picture or drawing of a dragon place it where it can be seen by all. You might also ask participants to draw pictures of a dragon. Ask them what thoughts and images come to mind when they think of dragons. Explain that some ancient cultures associated dragons with evil, while for others, Southeast Asians for example, the dragon was an image of reverence and hope. Give index cards to participants for writing their responses to the Scripture reading.

Getting Started

Leader: During Jesus' life many people were thought to be possessed by evil spirits. These were not dragons, but demons beyond their control. Think of some of the evils in our own age. Write some of these on the index card in front of you.

Speaker One: One of the most awesome characters in Christian tradition is Michael the Archangel. Part of Michael's story is found in the book of Revelation. There he is pictured driving a fire-breathing dragon, the "father of deceit," from heaven.

Speaker Two: Today science has dispelled our fear of dragons. None of us fears that a fire-breathing monster will break into this room to ravage all in sight.

Speaker Three: Although the fear of dragons is a thing of the past, the evil symbolized by the dragon in the Book of Revelation is still very much with us. Let us prepare our hearts to listen to a description of the great battle between the dragon and Michael.

Quiet Time

Reader One: A reading from the Book of Revelation 12:1-12: A great sign appeared in the sky...

Response

Leader: As sign of your willingness to fight evil, look at the evils you wrote on your index card, and write one way you can work to overcome these evils. (*When all have written, invite them to share these aloud.*)

Conclusion

Speaker Four: We are asked to battle the evils that destroy life, freedom, and humanity. Addictions to alcohol and drugs devour our own freedom, and destroy our relationships with God and others.

All: Lord, free us from evil.

Speaker Five: Poverty, hunger, homelessness, and greed destroy the quality of life for millions of people in our world.

All: Lord, free us from evil.

Speaker Six: The dragon of militarism puts weapons before people and teaches us to hate our sisters and brothers.

All: Lord, free us from evil.

Speaker Seven: Racism and sexism destroy the beauty of persons who were created in the image and likeness of God.

All: Lord, free us from evil.

Speaker Eight: Pollution is destroying our air, water, and the land of our Earth.

All: Lord, free us from evil.

Leader: Mighty God, and Michael, our protector, help us to be strong in our fight against evil. Comfort us with the knowledge that Jesus fights with us and will also help us in our struggle against evil until we share the victory he promises, life and joy with you forever.

All: Amen.

2

Prejudice:
A Different Way of Seeing

Times for Use

All Saints Day (November 1), Independence Day (July 4), Martin Luther King Day (mid-January), or any occasion that focuses on accepting differences among peoples.

Materials Needed

Pictures of people of various nationalities.

Introduction

People fear differences, and this is the basis of prejudice. In the United States today there are public assaults on Jews and black people, on Asians and Hispanics. How are we preparing our young people to overcome such prejudices? Are they simply to tolerate others or welcome them as equal brothers and sisters?

The message from Scripture is clear. We are all children of the one God. God's love does not discriminate. All people are created out of love, redeemed through the sacrificial love of Jesus, and called to discipleship and fullness of life with God. All life is a gift from God, and our faith leads us deeply into the mystery of our God's love.

Shared Experience

Post around your meeting area pictures of people of different nationalities. Ask the young people to look at these pictures and silently reflect about any prejudices they might feel. Ask if there are people at school they find it difficult to talk with. Remind them that most of us have prejudices, often because we do not associate with a particular group of people. The best way to overcome our prejudices is to admit that we have them and to get to know the people we find hard to accept.

Now ask each participant to sit next to someone he or she doesn't know very well. Ask them to get some basic information about their partners, for example name, age, hobby, favorite food, and some facts about their family life. Then have each pair introduce one another to the whole group.

Getting Started

Leader: Listen carefully to the following news stories.

Narrator: Extra, extra, read all about it.

Reader One: Hartford, Connecticut. A Jewish rabbi was found early this morning in a parking lot. He had broken ribs, a broken jaw, and blackened eyes. No money was missing when police found him. He was beaten and left for dead.

Jesus: Whatever you do to the least of my sisters or brothers you do to me.

Quiet Time

Reader Two: Providence, Rhode Island. A Spanish tenant of a rooming house was beaten with a baseball bat because of his Spanish origins.

Jesus: By your love for one another will all people know that you are my followers.

Quiet Time

Reader Three: Boston, Massachusetts. A Cambodian laborer and his family were evicted from their three-room apartment because their white neighbors complained about noise. There has been no evidence produced to support this charge.

Jesus: If you don't love your neighbor whom you can see, how can you possibly love God whom you do not see?

Quiet Time

Narrator: Why is it that we have such problems with people who are different? Why are we sometimes violent toward people we don't even know, or who disagree with us? Why are we afraid and insecure about ourselves? It is as if we hope to confirm our own goodness by attacking others. Instead of confronting our own faults, we attack them in others. How can we reconcile such actions with the example and teaching of Jesus?

Reader Four: On the night before he died Jesus shared with his friends his last thoughts. Just as we would only say what was most important to us if we knew we were going to die, Jesus saved what was most important to him until then. "Love one another as I have loved you," is what Jesus said.

Narrator: Jesus reminds us that if we are serious about following him, we need to love one another. There is no exception to this. Our differences can be a source of difficulty or a source of enrichment. We are asked by Jesus not just to *tolerate* those who are different from us, but to love them wholeheartedly. In this way we learn to know and accept others, and we become richer by doing this.

Response
All should stand in a circle. Invite each young person to place a hand on the shoulder of the person next to him or her.

Girl: Violence breeds violence but so does love breed love.

All: Lord, help us to love one another as you have loved us.

Boy: We will have conflicts, but let us resolve them using our intelligence, patience, creativity, and friendship.

All: Lord, help us to love one another as you have loved us.

Conclusion
Leader: Loving God, each day we can choose either prejudice or love. Help us to choose love, and to accept all others that we may be witnesses of Jesus.

All: Amen.

(*Invite participants to share a handshake or other sign of affection and respect.*)

3

Friendship: God's Gift to Us

Times for Use

Valentine'sDay (February 14), Holy Thursday, and any occasion when love and friendship are themes.

Materials Needed

A poster showing two joined hands or intertwined rings, paper, pencils, and a large dish.

Introduction

The world of friendship is sought by most young people. Friends can be trusted because they keep their word, laugh at our jokes, and cry with us in our sorrows. Friends, real friends, stand by us during our worst days as well as during our best days. They often share our dreams of the future and our secrets in the present. It is all too easy to take for granted those whom God has placed in our lives as friends. One of the most comfortable ways for teenagers to think of Jesus is as a friend.

Shared Experience

Place the poster with two hands joined in friendship or two rings intertwined in front of your group. Invite participants to think of their best friend, and to share something about this person with the group. Ask: What makes someone a friend? How do you think life would be without friendships? Allow time for response.

Getting Started

Leader: Let's reflect together on the importance of friendship.

Speaker One: Can you imagine what it would be like to live without friends?

Speaker Two: Imagine! No one to laugh at your jokes, no one to listen to your problems, no one with whom to share your secrets, no one to enter with you into your sadness and your joy.

Speaker One: To live without friends would be to live in a kind of hell.

Speaker Three: But friendship brings aches and pains as well as blessings. There are misunderstandings and power struggles and hurt feelings. There is the danger of conforming to what friends want even when we don't believe it's right. Each of us has probably suffered frustration because of our friends.

Quiet Time

Reader One: Let's listen together to the Word of God (Sirach 6:14-17, adapted) to discover what it says about friendship:

A faithful friend is a sturdy shelter. The person who finds one finds a treasure.

Reader Two: A faithful friend is beyond price; no sum can balance her worth.

Reader One: A faithful friend is a life-saving remedy; so also is the one who fears God.

Reader Two: For the one who fears God follows God's ways; so, too, his friend.

Response

Leader: Scripture says friends are a treasure, but do we look upon our friends as treasures? Do we treat them with reverence and respect, or do we try to control them or take them for granted?

(At this point ask participants to write the names of their friends on small pieces of paper and place these on a dish at the front of the room.)

Conclusion

Leader: *(Holding high the dish with the names)* Lord, we thank you for the gift of friendship.

All:	Lord, we thank you for the gift of friendship.
Leader:	Forgive us for taking our friends for granted.
All:	Lord, we thank you for the gift of friendship.
Leader:	Holy God, loving mother and wise father, you have given us Jesus as our brother and friend. Help us never to take his friendship for granted, but may each of our friendships draw us closer to him and to you.
All:	Amen.

4

True Happiness: Being Myself

Times for Use

All Saints Day (November 1), during confirmation preparation, and any occasion on which self-acceptance is the theme.

Materials Needed

A large mirror or hand mirror, used magazines and newspapers, scissors, glue, pencils and paper.

Introduction

We live in a society that attempts to reduce everything to a commodity. Even intangible values are associated with products. For example, a car can bring you real freedom, perfume or after-shave can guarantee the perfect relationship, name-brand clothes can bring happiness. The message of advertising is that people are not good enough the way they are. To improve their physical and emotional imperfections they must buy the latest fad in clothes, cars, or cosmetics. That others want the same thing they want only makes it more valuable and their need to own it is supported therefore by the crowd.

The message of the gospel is quite different. We are imperfect, true, but to be perfectly human is to learn to live with this imperfection. We should, of course, try to improve ourselves, but our real source of strength is God. Our imperfection stems from our split with God through sin. Only an ongoing conversion to Christ in faith and dependence on the grace of God and God's mercy will allow us to overcome sin and evil.

Shared Experience

Place a large mirror in a conspicuous place where participants will have to walk past it. You might also walk by the young people with a mirror in your hand and ask each to look at him or herself in the mirror. Have advertisements placed around the room or if time permits let the young make collages of advertisements and place these around the room.

Discuss with participants the effect of some of the advertising they experience each day. Ask them why companies spend so much money advertising to try and sell their products. What is the message of advertising? Aren't many advertisements telling us in one way or another that we are no good the way we are, that only if we buy their product will we become happy or free or rich or successful? Advertising constantly plays on our insecurities, our shortcomings in order to create dissatisfaction in us so we will buy more and more.

Explain that this is one reason it was hard for some of them to look in the mirror. They believe they are just not good enough. They can't accept themselves as they are and don't like looking at themselves. Ask them to keep these ideas in mind as you now ask God to help them accept themselves just as God does.

Getting Started

Speaker One: I assume most of us look into a mirror at one point or another after we get up in the morning. When you look into a mirror do you like what you see? I believe for many of us the answer is no. We find it difficult to love ourselves the way we are.

Speaker Two: Many of us are hard on ourselves. We put ourselves down, exaggerating our shortcomings and failures while refusing to accept the compliments of others.

Speaker Three: Advertisements play into our insecurities. We are constantly told by advertisements that we are no good the way we are. We are commanded to look at our imperfections and to fix ourselves up by buying the latest in fashion, food and entertainment. Happiness will come after we wear the latest hair style, use the freshest mouthwash and sprinkle ourselves with the most seductive cologne or aftershave. Happiness and really loving ourselves is always just out of reach, but it will surely be ours with the next purchase.

Quiet Time

Speaker Four: How different is Jesus' view of us, how refreshing his message. Let's listen to his word to us from sacred Scripture.

Reader One:	A reading from the gospel of Luke (12:22-31): He said to his disciples, "That is why I warn you, do not be concerned for your life, what you are to eat, or for your body, what you are to wear..."

Response

Leader:	Ask each person to write a slogan that will remind him or her that they can't be "bought." The slogan should in some way bring out the truth that what we need for happiness is already within ourselves. The task is to discover the treasure within ourselves rather than try to purchase a perishable trinket. For example, I may be shy but I'm a great listener, or I'm not a great student but I sure am a great friend, or happiness can't be bought only discovered within. These slogans can be kept in a safe place at home where the young people can refer to them when they need a reminder.

Conclusion

(The parts identified for left and right side may also be read by individual people.)

Leader:	Jesus does not ask us to be perfect, which is impossible, but to become compassionate, which is the human way and necessary for a happy life. Jesus comes to us from God loving us while we are still sinners, still imperfect. This is the story of the Lost Son, the Lost Sheep and the Lost Coin. It is also the story of the young person on drugs, or sexually exploited or alienated from family or friends. The gospel, the good news, is your story and mine.
Left Side:	Jesus, you invite us to love ourselves as we are because you love us.
All:	Teach us, Lord, that happiness lies within.
Right Side:	Jesus, you invite us to seek happiness the only place it can be found, within our own hearts.
All:	Teach us, Lord, that happiness lies within.
Left Side:	Help us, Lord, to learn to be friends with ourselves and to seek to understand ourselves better, that we may love ourselves more completely.

All:	Teach us, Lord, that happiness lies within.
Left Side:	Jesus, you invite us to see ourselves and others through your eyes.
All:	Teach us, Lord, that happiness lies within.
Leader:	Help us, Lord, to be free from the illusion that happiness comes from outside of ourselves and acceptance comes from being perfect. Rather, help us accept ourselves as you accept us and love others with the love you have for each of us. We pray in Jesus' name.
All:	Amen.

5

God: Our Holy Mother

Times for Use

Feast of the Annunciation (March 25), Mother's Day (second week in May), and any occasion on which God's parental love is the theme.

Materials Needed

A picture of Mary, small pictures of mothers, paper, pencils, newsprint, and markers.

Introduction

Most of us are accustomed to calling God our Father. When Jesus prayed, he named God with the informal "Abba," which means daddy. In sharing his prayer with his disciples he shared his own relationship with God. He certainly wasn't denoting a sexual identity to God for God transcends sexuality. Rather he was praying out of his experience and naming that experience with the best language available to him at that time and place. But God is equally our mother.

Pope John Paul the First called attention to this when he stated, "We know that God never takes an eye off us, even if all is dark around us. God is Father, better yet: God is Mother, who wants only the best for her own, for all her own. And when children are sick, they, more than others, have a right to their mother's love."

Perhaps the best known descriptions of God as mother come from the fourteenth-century spiritual writer, Lady Julian of Norwich. She describes God as the wisdom and loving kindness of motherhood. In Scripture God is pictured as giving birth to her people and caring for them like a mother cares for her child. Mary, whom we name the mother of God, is a clear reflection of God's own motherhood.

The names we use to express our relationship with God often find resonance in the way we relate with one another. It is important to reclaim the truth of God's motherhood without in any way denying God's presence as "Abba."

Shared Experience

Begin by placing a large picture of Mary, the Madonna, in a visible place. Surround this with smaller pictures of mothers carrying out various aspects of their vocation. Invite participants to fold a piece of paper in half. On one half ask them to print the word "Mother" at the top and under it list all the characteristics and qualities they associate with motherhood. On the other half, ask them to print the word "Father" at the top and under it all the characteristics they associate with fatherhood. Allow them time to share these with one another. You may want to list some of these qualities on a poster or blackboard.

Ask participants if they ever think of God as mother. Have them refer to their papers and point out that God has all the characteristics of both mother and father. This truth is verified in the existence of two sexes both created in the image of God. It is true that Jesus called God Father and daddy. That was how the language and culture of his day permitted him to speak of God. But God is not only strong and powerful, characteristics we often associate with fatherhood. God is also wise, compassionate, and understanding, characteristics often associated with motherhood.

Getting Started

Leader: We are going to pray now, focusing on the motherhood of God. This is important to help us to know God more completely and to help us to know that motherhood is just as important as fatherhood. When we pray to God only as father, we tend to think that authority, one of God's characteristics, belongs only to men. If we always name God "father," we tend to think that women are second-class citizens who share none of God's qualities.

So, let us begin. In the name of God who is Father, and Mother and Holy Spirit, Amen. Loving God, you have created us in your image and likeness. Help us to know you both as a strong, protecting father and as a wise compassionate mother. We pray this in the name of Jesus your son.

All: Amen.

Quiet Time

Reader One: As we listen to this adapted reading from Isaiah the prophet (66:10–13), let us recall that God loves us with a motherly love:

Rejoice with Jerusalem and be glad all you who love her, all you who were mourning over her. Oh that you may suck fully of the milk of her comfort, that you might nurse with delight at her abundant breast.

Reader Two: As children you will be carried in her arms and fondled in her lap; as a mother comforts her child, so will I comfort you. The word of the Lord.

All: Thanks be to God.

Response
Invite participants to now write a prayer addressing God as Mother. For example: Loving God, our Mother, you give us life, nourish us with your love and comfort us in times of sorrow. Amen. Appropriate background music may be played during this response.

Conclusion

Speaker One: All of us are created in your image, God. Help us to know you as both a loving mother and a strong, understanding father.

All: God, you are motherly. You are fatherly. We praise you.

Speaker Two: All of us are created in your image, God. We seek to be wise, compassionate, and protecting of the weak and poor, like you. But also like you, we need to be strong, courageous, and unselfish to fight injustice and violence.

All: God, you are motherly. You are fatherly. Help us to know you.

Speaker Three: All of us are born from a mother's love. Mary, a perfect model of the motherhood of God, said yes to the invitation to give birth to the Christ child. Help us to love our mothers and to protect all mothers who give new life to our world.

All: God, you are motherly. You are fatherly. Help us to make you known by being full of strength and compassion in our everyday lives. Amen.

(You might want to allow time for the young people to write short letters of appreciation to their mothers to take home after this gathering.)

6

Stewardship:
Earth Is Our Mother

Times for Use

Feast of Francis of Assisi (October 4), Earth Day or Arbor Day (both celebrated in the spring), and any occasion on which caring for Earth is the theme.

Materials Needed

Newsprint, markers, and copies of Psalm 104. Optional: pictures of nature scenes, a large poster of Earth, and pictures of Native Americans.

Introduction

Christians live in daily anticipation of the Parousia, the final coming of Christ. For this reason every age and season is for the Christian the final age, the last times. And yet, Christians also have responsibility for what happens in this present day and age.

Perhaps the "happening" most familiar to our young people today is the ecological movement. The depletion of the ozone layer, global warming, deforestation of the rain forest, pollution of our oceans and rivers, and chemical poisoning of the air we breathe, all call us to take responsibility for Earth. As Christians we are invited to view creation as a sacred expression of the creator. In this we are very close to Native American spirituality. Our young know that caring for the environment is the necessary thing to do. Through prayer they can experience care for Earth as a way to love God and protect the life that reflects God's presence.

Shared Experience

If possible, conduct this service in a park, at a beach, or some other place where teenagers can experience the beauty and order of nature. Make the environment the focus of this service. If it's not possible to go to a natural setting, place pictures of trees, water, and animals around the room. Place a large poster of Earth in a central location. You might also include pictures of Native Americans.

Ask participants what they know about the ecological crisis, and allow them to share responses. Invite them to look at protecting the environment as a way to show their love for God. Ask if they have ever thought of creation and nature as expressing God's presence and care for them, and therefore as sacred things. Invite them, in groups of three or four, to reflect on their ordinary day and list on newsprint the natural resources they depend on to live. Remind them to include such things as sunlight, air, and clean water. Next have them list ways they might be abusing Earth's resources.

Getting Started

Leader:	As we begin our prayer I invite you to think about creation. Are you "part of creation" or "separate from creation"? *(You might want to put these phrases on a poster for all to see.)* Are the resources of Earth something you feel power over, or do you experience yourself as part of your environment? Do you treat the environment as something fragile to be treasured, knowing that how you treat it will eventually reflect back on your life?
Reader One:	Being part of creation is central to Native American spirituality. Listen to these words of Chief Seattle of the Susquamish tribe: "Every part of this earth is sacred to my people. Every shining pine needle, every sandy shore, every mist in the dark woods, every clearing and humming insect is holy in the memory and experience of my people. The sap which courses through the trees carries memories of the red man. How can you buy or sell the sky, the warmth of the land? The idea is strange to us."
Reader Two:	"The rivers are our brothers, and they quench our thirst. The rivers carry our canoes and feed our children. If we sell you our land, you must remember and teach your children that the rivers are our brothers and yours, and you must henceforth give the rivers the kindness you would give any brother."
Reader Three:	"The air is precious to the red man, for all things share the same breath—the beast, the tree, the man, they all share the same breath."

Quiet Time

Leader: Let us listen to how God found joy in creation. An adapted reading from Genesis (1:14-31): God made two great lights, the greater one to govern the day and the lesser one to govern the night.... Then God said, "Let the waters teem with an abundance of living creatures, and on earth let the birds fly below the dome of the sky. Let the earth bring forth all kinds of living creatures, cattle, creeping things, and wild animals of all kinds." God saw how good it was and blessed them. The word of the Lord.

All: Thanks be to God.

Response
Ask participants to jot down one practical, specific thing they can do to protect the environment. Allow them to share this information with the person next to them.

Conclusion
Speaker One: Let us join in prayer to ask God's forgiveness for times we have abused Earth and for the wisdom to love and care for her.

Left Side: For times we waste food, water, and electricity, we pray to the Lord.

All: Lord, have mercy on us.

Right Side: For times we think Earth is ours to dominate and do with as we wish, we pray.

All: Lord, have mercy on us.

Left Side: For the wisdom to realize that Earth and its resources belong to all God's people to be shared fairly, we pray.

All: Lord, have mercy on us.

Right Side: For the ability to experience oneness with creation and to be filled with respect and gratitude for the gifts of God's love, we pray.

All: Lord, have mercy on us.

                *(You may want to add items from the lists of abuses prepared dur-
                ing the Shared Experience.)*

All: Loving God, help us to love and protect Earth and teach us
                to love you by respecting, sharing and caring for your crea-
                tion. Amen.

                *(Before closing, give each person a copy of Psalm 104 to read at
                home.)*

Note: The quotes from Chief Seattle are taken from *The Christian Call to Justice and Peace* by Joseph
Stoutzenberger (Saint Mary's Press).

7

Peace: Discovering God's Way

Times for Use

January 1 (which is now designated as a World Day of Peace), Good Friday, and any occasion on which there are conflicts to resolve.

Materials Needed

A cross, a picture of a dove, a spotlight, small felt doves or crosses, pictures for a collage, scissors and glue, pencils, and the following four signs: 1) I'm Number One, 2) My world is okay, 3) I earned it, it's mine, 4) Peace is for some people only.

Introduction

Peace! Peace now. Peace with honor. Peace be with you. For some peace seems to be the absence of violence or war. For others it is the tranquility of mind that results when all is well in their world. Still others experience peace as victory over an opponent.

But peace in the Christian tradition is much more than all these. It results when people live in harmony with one another, with their natural environment, and with God. Peace comes not with victory or conquest, but when we show mutual respect for our sisters and brothers everywhere in the world. For the Christian, peace is rooted in Christ and his way of forgiveness and reconciliation. Christ is our peace. We are his ambassadors.

Shared Experience

Place a cross or the picture of a dove in the center of the room with a spotlight on it. Explain that the cross is a sign of peace, as is the dove. Place small felt doves or crosses on the table. Ask participants if they understand the meaning of these symbols. If time permits, ask them to make collages that illustrate what peace means to them. Or simply invite them to take a moment and reflect on what peace means to them.

After a short time, ask them to write answers to the following questions: Who is a person of peace? Is there something in your personality that blocks your efforts to be peaceful in your relationships and attitudes towards others? Explain.

After writing, invite them to reflect on their own responses.

Getting Started

Speaker One: (Holding a sign that reads, "I'm number one.") What is peace for me? It's a feeling I get when I win an argument, or when what I want to do gets done.

Speaker Two: (Holding a sign that reads, "My world is O.K.") Peace is me feeling tranquil and calm. I know there are kids who are in pain, who are without friends and who feel left out, but that's not my business. As long as my world is undisturbed, I am at peace.

Speaker Three: (Holding a sign that reads: "I earned it, it's mine.") I know there are people who are hungry and homeless, but peace to me means I have a right to what I earn. If I want to buy more clothes than I need or waste food, that's nobody's business but mine. I'm not bothering anyone, so leave me in peace.

Speaker Four: (Holding a sign that reads: "Peace is for some people only.") I try to get along with most kids. It's just the blacks and the Hispanics I can't stomach. Otherwise, I'm very much at peace.

Quiet Time

Leader: Let us listen to Saint Paul's words to the Corinthians (2 Cor. 5:17-21, adapted): Those who are in Christ are a new creation. We have been reconciled with God through Christ. God is not counting our sins against us, but has entrusted us with the message of reconciliation. The word of the Lord.

All: Thanks be to God.

Leader: The peace of Jesus is not "getting our way," but seeking what is fair and just. Jesus offers the peace of reconciliation, of making whole what is broken through forgiveness. As the Father loves Jesus, he loves us and invites us to bring his love to each person we meet.

Response
(You might want to play soft music.) Invite participants to reflect on the cross as a sign of God's strong love and the dove as a sign of God's gentle love. Invite them to come forward and take either a cross or a dove, whichever they need most to be peaceful.

Conclusion

Leader: Let us now pray for peace.

Right Side: For safety of body and spirit.

All: God, grant us peace.

Left Side: For peace that is rooted in the belief that Jesus is our peace...

All: God, grant us peace.

Right Side: For the conviction that Jesus has removed the walls that separate one people, one race from another...

All: God, grant us peace.

Left Side: That we may never call hatred patriotism...

All: God, grant us peace.

Right Side: That we might seek just relations among all peoples, and fairly share Earth's resources...

All: God, grant us peace.

Leader: May the Holy Spirit of love bless us with hope and may we be filled with the peace of Christ.

All: Amen.

(Now all should share some sign of peace.)

8

Hide and Seek:
God Invites Us to Freedom

Times for Use
Advent, Lent, when preparing for confirmation, or as immediate preparation for the sacrament of reconciliation.

Materials Needed
A container of water, a statue of Mary or one of the saints, and a piece of cloth.

Introduction
Most teenagers have at one time played the game of hide and seek. It's a good metaphor for their lives. They seek happiness in many ways: success in school and athletics, companionship through dating, and adventure and excitement through parties, trips, and concerts. But sometimes what they seek leads them into experiences they regret. They might cheat on a test, use people sexually, get drunk at a party, or become involved with drugs or gang violence. They feel ashamed and guilty and they hide.

It is into their places of hiding that God, who is their true friend, journeys with them. There in their shame God loves them and invites them to face their failure, to trust in God's forgiveness, and to begin again on the right path.

When others condemn us and see only our failure and sin, Jesus looks into our hearts, our center, and invites us out of hiding back to the path of love and life, where we celebrate the mystery of God's love and forgiveness.

Shared Experience
Place a container of water in a central place. If possible cover with a cloth a statue of a saint, one who is familiar to your group, for example Mary, the mother of Jesus, Joseph, Patrick or Francis of Assisi. Ask

participants if they have ever played hide and seek. Did they like it better to hide or to find those hiding? After they have a chance to respond, invite them to remember a time when hiding was more for them than a childhood game.

For example, can they remember a time they "hid" even from friends or parents because they were ashamed? What was it like to feel ashamed enough to want to hide? Although it may be difficult, invite anyone who wants to, to share their experiences. Point out that it is at times like these that only someone who really cares for us can see beyond our sin and shame into our hearts to the real us.

Getting Started

Leader: When, as small children, we played hide and seek, it was great fun to sometimes find friends who were hiding and sometimes let them find us.

Speaker One: Life is a lot like this. Most of us are seeking people, things, and events in life that will make us happy. We are all seekers in one way or another.

Speaker Two: Sometimes we seek love in relationships, sometimes knowledge through study. Sometimes our goal is to be successful in the drama club or on the soccer field. Sometimes we seek meaning in career planning. It is through seeking that we discover who we are, our values, beliefs and dreams.

Speaker Three: It's good to remember this when we pray to God. God, too, is a seeker who is trying to find us. The message of Christ is that God is relentless in searching for us. God follows us not only into our places of success, where we are happy to be recognized, but also into our places of hiding, where we are filled with shame and guilt. When others leave us because they see something disgusting, God stands by us and sees the inner person.

Quiet Time

Reader One: Close your eyes now and listen to a reading from the gospel of John (John 8:3-11): The scribes and Pharisees led a woman forward who had been caught in the act of adultery…

(After the reading you might want to note that the man, too, was guilty, but in the society of that time the woman alone was publicly blamed. This is a grave injustice.)

Response

This would be an appropriate time to celebrate the sacrament of reconciliation. Explain that those who would like to allow Jesus to come into their hiding places, their places of shame, can now take advantage of the sacrament of God's forgiving presence.

(After celebrating the sacrament of reconciliation, or if the sacrament is not being celebrated, invite a volunteer to come forward to remove the cloth from the statue.)

Leader: The saints were always able to come out of hiding because they believed that Christ's truth had set them free. We, too, can believe that Christ has set us free. We, too, can come out of hiding. In the waters of baptism we received this gift of freedom. Let us now use water as a sign of God's love for us.

(Ask participants to come forward and form a circle. The first dips her hand into the water and makes the sign of the cross on the forehead of the next person in the circle saying, "Come out of hiding, God loves you." Continue until all have received this blessing.)

Conclusion

Leader: Go now in peace, knowing that God loves and forgives you and always seeks you out. May you seek and find God in all your daily activities. Amen.

9

Saying Thank You:
The Meaning of Eucharist

Times for Use

Thanksgiving, the Feast of Corpus Christi, and any occasion on which Eucharist is the theme.

Materials Needed

Wheat, grapes, a loaf of bread, a list containing the words "thank you" in as many languages as possible, construction paper, scissors, and tape.

Introduction

For the follower of Christ, to give thanks is as natural as breathing. Jesus gave thanks constantly and so must we. Jesus praised God for food when he fed the large crowd with bread and fishes, as well as at the last meal he shared with his friends. He thanked God for the faith of the humble and for revealing to little ones the secrets of the kingdom. He thanked God for little children whom he blessed, and the birds of the air and fish of the sea whom he used in his parables.

What is thanks if not an attitude toward life that recognizes we are all connected to one another in mysterious ways? Giving thanks binds us to one another. It respects the fact that all of us are dependent on each other for life and sustenance. Each of us is part of a much larger mystery. Thanksgiving is rooted in the awareness that God is present in our lives. Jesus invites us to enter into his own eucharist, his feast of thanksgiving, to celebrate the abundant generosity of God.

Shared Experience

Place on a table pieces of wheat, some grapes, and a loaf of bread. Any one of these symbols is sufficient. Have the young people cut out the letters for the words "thank you" in various languages and place these in the front of the room on a poster.

Ask the young people to name one thing or person for whom they are thankful. Ask if it is easy or difficult for them to say thank you. Ask how a hostage recently returned from captivity might experience gratitude for freedom in a way distinct from themselves. How might a survivor of a serious automobile accident experience gratitude for health?

Illustrate how indebted we are to each other through the following simple exercise. Let the young people look at the tags in the lining of their shirt collars. Let them name the various places their shirts or sweaters were made. Recognizing their interdependence on others in the world is a big part of gratitude.

Getting Started

Speaker One: I'm tired of being around people who are selfish. It's not much fun. "It's mine, what's in it for me, I earned it, I'm going to take care of number one." These are the attitudes and thoughts that accompany selfishness. I'm sick of it.

Speaker Two: It's easy for all of us to be self-centered. We live in a society that tells us selfishness is a virtue, a strength. Independence is so emphasized that we forget we are also interdependent. I believe when we are awake to our relatedness we will also awaken to life. We will never be bored or boring. But it's easy to take others for granted. It's easy to fall asleep to the beauty and richness of the world that God has entrusted to us. We forget that life is a gift to us. We think we deserve it.

Speaker Three: I believe that the happiness which we all seek is not so much found in getting what we want as in finding a new reason to be grateful every day of our lives. What about you? What do you think?

Quiet Time

Reader One: Let us listen together to hear the importance of thanksgiving in the life of Jesus. A reading from the gospel of Mark (14:22-25): During the meal Jesus took bread…

Leader: As followers of Christ we are people of the eucharist, the meal of thanksgiving. Bread and wine are symbols of Jesus' gift of himself in the eucharist. Jesus gave thanks to God before his suffering and death. He made clear for us that thanksgiving is not about feeling good or owning possessions or having things our way. In giving thanks, Jesus recognized his connectedness to God from whom all things come.

Even in the face of death Jesus realized that union with God was the root of thanksgiving. Thanksgiving is the light that shines from our eyes when we recognize that every breath we take is a gift. Every minute we live is a gift entrusted to us by a loving God. We are all connected by these gifts to God and to one another.

Response

Leader: Invite the young people to stand in a circle. Ask them to join hands as a sign of their dependence on one another. Ask them to name one person or thing for which they are thankful. For example: "For my family I am thankful." Then all can respond, "We thank you, Lord."

(If the group has difficulty, suggest the following:)
For our lives and for the lives of those who love us...

All: We thank you, Lord.

Leader: For the gift of health...

All: We thank you, Lord.

Leader: For the gifts of food, shelter, and clothing...

All: We thank you, Lord.

Leader: For the gift of our minds and our bodies...

All: We thank you, Lord.

Leader: For all our gifts and talents...

All: We thank you, Lord.

Conclusion

Leader: Holy Spirit, you invite all of us into a mystery of love beyond our understanding. Teach us to give thanks.

All:	Amen.
Leader:	Inspire us to be humble and full of gratitude. May every meal we share remind us of our connectedness to God and to one another.
All:	Amen.
Leader:	And may your blessing be on us in the name of the Father, Mother God, Son, and Holy Spirit.
All:	Amen.

10

Self-Esteem:
Becoming the Hands of God

Times for Use
New Year's Day, the first week of a new school year, the birthday of one of the participants, and any occasion on which self-esteem is the topic.

Materials Needed
Tragedy/comedy masks, pencils and paper.

Introduction
The self-esteem of our teenagers is greatly influenced by the opinions and comments of their peers. Although they say they don't care what others think, their actions reveal a different side. One criticism amid ten compliments is what they remember. Even a passing remark of a critical nature causes secret doubts and hidden insecurities. Perhaps at no other time in their lives do the opinions of others carry so much weight as during teenage years.

This gives the young tremendous power over each other. We need to nurture their ability to feel good about themselves, without the need to put another down. We have to point out how their comments can affect one another for good or for evil. Above all, we have to show them the connection between loving themselves and loving others, and help them to see their call to participate in making the kingdom of God present through their acts of love.

Shared Experience
Place a picture or drawing of a drama mask for tragedy and comedy in a central place. Ask participants to recall the last time someone criticized them. What was the criticism and how did they feel about it? To

help them along, give each a sheet of paper with the word or symbol for comedy at the top of one column and the word or symbol for tragedy at the head of the other. Ask them to list under the tragedy column all the put-downs and criticisms received in the past week. Under the comedy column all the compliments. Then ask them to indicate how they felt when criticized or complimented. Sad, angry, happy, joyful, depressed or hopeful are some of the words they can use. Ask them to keep these lists handy.

Getting Started

Leader: The things we say and do to one another and the way we resolve conflicts have a profound effect on how each of us sees ourselves and feels about ourselves. If we have low self-esteem because of being criticized, it will be harder to reach out to and love others. On a deeper level, how we treat others reflects not only how we feel about ourselves but also our belief or lack of belief in God. The story you are about to hear will help point this out.

Speaker One: Have you heard the story of the soldier in Italy during World War II who found a statue of Jesus in a village? The statue was in pieces. The soldier, who was an artist, tried to fix the statue. He was able to fix everything but the hands. He left the statue at the center of town with a note around its neck. The note said: "I am Jesus. I have no hands in the world now but yours."

Quiet Time

Reader One: As we picture the statue of Jesus, let us listen to a paraphrased reading from the first letter of John (4:7, 19, 21):

My friends let us love one another because love is of God. The person who loves is God's child and really knows God. If any one of us says we love God whom we can't see while hating the person next to us, we are liars. Whoever really loves God also loves their sisters and brothers. The word of the Lord.

Response

Leader: We, like the statue of Jesus, are broken when people criticize us or put us down. It is very hard for us to love them. In order to overcome our sensitivity to this criticism, we need to focus on our gifts and talents.

34

I would like you to think of something you do well or one of your best qualities. This is not bragging. Bragging is exaggerating your gifts. It is a good thing to know and take ownership of the gifts God has given you.

(You may need to give examples such as: I'm a good listener, I'm a good friend, I draw well, I have a nice smile. Ask each person to share one of his or her good points with the group. Although this may be hard for some, it is of great importance.)

Conclusion

Leader: Let us conclude our prayer together.

Left Side: Each of us can give others feelings of rejection and worthlessness or feelings of acceptance and belonging. No one has ever seen God.

All: Yet, if we love one another, God dwells in us.

Right Side: A simple "Hello" or "It's okay" or "Will you forgive me?" can begin a process of new life that brings healing to ourselves and others. No one can see God.

All: Yet, if we love one another, God dwells in us.

Left Side: I wonder who teaches us never to admit we are wrong, or that we have to win an argument, or that yelling and fighting are better than listening and reasoning and trying to peacefully seek the truth? No one can see God.

All: Yet, if we love one another, God dwells in us.

Right side: When was the last time we said, "I love you," and really meant it?

All: If we love one another, God dwells in us and in our world.

(If the group is small enough, invite each member to come forward. Place your hands on each forehead saying: "Remember, Christ now has no hands but yours. Go in peace.")

11

Sexuality: It's About Love

Times for Use

Advent, Valentine's Day, during a weekend retreat, and any occasion on which dating and relationships are the theme.

Materials Needed

Pictures of athletes, rock stars, and TV and movie stars, newsprint, markers, paper and pencils.

Introduction

Adolescence is a confusing time when physical, emotional, and psychological changes are occurring. Often the messages given to the young about growing up and especially about sexuality add to their confusion. Nowhere is the challenge facing them and the need for wise guidance more evident than in the area of sexuality. The pressure from the media and its heroes often present selfish models of sexual behavior, people who take no personal responsibility for consequences to themselves or others. Peer pressure and the culture as a whole (along with the frequent lack of parental guidance in the area of sexuality), leave the young to deal on their own with sexual feelings and their need for affection. Clearly sexuality is a gift from God and sexual activity is not just something we do but an expression of who we are as persons. When we invite our young people to become fully human and fully alive, we can help them direct their energies, including their sexuality, toward loving and serving others.

It would be helpful to ask participants if they understand the difference between sex and sexuality. You might suggest that sex is our gender, male or female, and sexuality embraces our whole person: body, emotions, mind, imagination, and will, everything that makes us unique. Problems arise when we treat sexuality as belonging to the body alone. For example, loving someone involves our mind (we must get to know them); our will (we must choose freely to be with them); our emotions (we must share feelings and active concern for them); and our imagination (we must be able to share our future plans, our dreams, and our fears with them). Having sex with someone can be simply a physical response to sexual feelings, and might have nothing to do with love. To become fully human, we need to direct all of our drives to the service of love.

Shared Experience

Place pictures of athletes, rock stars, or TV and film personalities in a visible place. If possible, place the words sex, sexuality, affection, self-esteem, and love around the room. Explain to participants that during this service they will be praying for a greater understanding of sexuality.

First, however, ask them to respond to this word association game. Tell them you are going to say a word and they are to say the first word that comes to mind. You may use any words to get them started. Include the words sex, sexuality, love, and God. Write these words on a piece of newsprint and place their responses beneath them. Discuss the ideas they associate with these terms.

Getting Started

Leader: Let's imagine we are eavesdropping on a teacher who is reading stories about sex in the daily paper.

Teacher: Former basketball player Wilt Chamberlain boasts of the number of women he has had sex with. Why would anyone brag about that?

(Pause.)

Teacher: Look at this, Magic Johnson says he is going to start encouraging safe sex. I suppose this means wearing a condom prevents the spread of AIDS. But sexuality is so much more than this. I can't believe what I'm reading.

(Pause.)

Teacher: Isn't it sad that the mystery of our sexual identity, our way of communicating our affection and love to each other, our way of joining in a joy-filled union to bring life into the world has been reduced to a drive, an instinct associated with disease, using people as playthings and fearing teenage pregnancy? Shouldn't there really be a much deeper message, one that deals with sexuality, and not just sexual acts? Why did God give us the gift of sexuality?

Quiet Time

Leader: Let's listen to words from Scripture that shed light on our dignity as human beings and children of God (to be read slowly and dramatically with long pauses between each): Do to others what you want others to do to you *(pause)*. Glorify God with your body *(pause)*. You are the dwelling place of God's Holy Spirit *(pause)*.

Response
Ask participants to think about their own sexuality. Invite them to make one or two resolutions to help them use their sexuality with respect and to treat others with respect. For example: I resolve to respect my body and to use it in loving service for God and others, or, I resolve to think about consequences before I act. Allow sufficient time for this, and then invite them to write these resolutions out and keep them at home to read and pray over.

Conclusion

Leader: Whenever our instincts control us, some kind of death follows, whether it be physical, emotional, or moral. We should be guided, not by instinct, but by values. If we want to be fully human, values such as fidelity, commitment, the ability to say no to ourselves, and to sacrifice for those we love will accompany us on our way.

Advocating the use of condoms to prevent AIDS does not address our Christian call to be whole persons or to relate to others responsibly.

Left Side: Loving God, you invite us to become fully human, compassionate, joy-filled people.

Right Side: Whether we will learn to become human and celebrate our sexuality or whether we relate to each other with fear and selfishness is our choice.

All: What great trust God has in us.

Left Side: Loving God, you are like a loving mother and a caring father to us. You have created us female and male in your image.

Right Side: We give you thanks for the gift of our sexuality. Help us to really know and love ourselves.

All: Teach us to live by your Spirit, Jesus, and direct our efforts to truly love others. Amen.

12

Forgiveness:
A Light in the Darkness

Times for Use
Lent, Holy Week, when preparing to receive the sacrament of reconciliation, and on any occasion when there are conflicts within the group.

Materials Needed
One large candle and five small candles.

Introduction
If there is one indispensable quality of Christian living, it is forgiveness. If there is one essential element that marks the heart and soul of the disciple more than any other, it is forgiveness. If there is one unquestionable characteristic of the Life Giver, the Anointed One, The Christ, it is forgiveness. Mercy and forgiveness are expressed often in the words of Jesus. Our Christian message to the world must be forgiveness, for our God is forgiving and rich in mercy.

Shared Experience
Have one person light a candle in the center of the assembly. Call attention to the light. Invite the young people to think of their relationships in terms of the light. When they have disagreements, arguments, or conflicts, the light of their relationships dim or go out. When a relationship is broken we have a choice to allow it to end or to work toward healing. There are some relationships that must end, for example where abuse is involved. But even though there is hurt in some relationships, hurt to those we love, the relationship can be healed. Forgiveness is the light that can get such a relationship going again.

Getting Started

Leader: Think of someone who has hurt you, but who really and sincerely wants forgiveness. Or, think of a relationship that ended because you or someone else could not offer forgiveness. How do you feel when someone forgives you? Ask yourself whether you are a forgiving person. Let's bring these thoughts and questions to prayer.

Speaker One: The black minister stood in front of his charred house. The night before, a fire bomb had been thrown through the window. He and his family escaped harm. When asked if he hated those who had attacked his family in such a vicious manner, he responded that he had seen too much of hate and what it does to ever want to hate anyone. These are the words of Martin Luther King., Jr.

Speaker Two: Forgiveness is never easy, but it is necessary. When one person in a relationship hurts another, but is too proud or fearful to ask forgiveness, the relationship crumbles. When I am the one who needs to forgive, but I withhold forgiveness from the one seeking it, the relationship ends. Because we sometimes harm the people we love, forgiveness is a necessary ingredient in any relationship. This is also true of society, and of relationships between peoples and nations. Life without forgiveness would be hell.

Speaker Three: Perhaps this is why Jesus made forgiveness and mercy characteristics of those who would be his disciples. We are invited to forgive not seven times but seventy times seven. It is the prodigal or lost child who brings joy to his father by seeking forgiveness. It is the publican whose simple prayer, "Lord, have mercy on me, a sinner," is heard by God.

Quiet Time

Reader One: A reading from the gospel of Luke (15:11-31): Jesus said to them, "A man had two sons..."

Response

Leader: Invite five members of the group forward as representatives of the whole gathering. Handing a lit candle to the first representative, you say, "Jesus offers us forgiveness as a light to heal broken relationships."

Student One:	*(Holding the candle)* Jesus, you say to me tonight that I am the lost son, the one who needs forgiveness seventy times seven.
All:	Lord, help us to seek forgiveness.
Leader:	*(Handing a lit candle to Student Two)* Jesus offers us forgiveness as a light to heal broken relationships.
Student Two:	Jesus, help us to experience our own need for forgiveness before each other and before our God.
All:	Lord, help us to offer forgiveness to others.
Leader:	*(Handing a lit candle to Student Three)* Jesus offers us forgiveness as a light to heal broken relationships.
Student Three:	Jesus, help us to become persons of healing.
All:	Lord, help us to offer forgiveness to others.
Leader:	*(Handing a candle to Student Four)* Jesus offers us forgiveness as a light to heal broken relationships.
Student Four:	Loving God, you have touched us with forgiveness over and over through the generous love of Jesus, your anointed one.
All:	Lord, help us to offer forgiveness to others.
Leader:	*(Handing a lit candle to Student Five)* Jesus offers us forgiveness as a light to heal broken relationships.
Student Five:	Help us to be true disciples offering forgiveness to those who need it from us and courageously seeking it from those we have harmed.
All:	Lord, help us to offer forgiveness to others.
Leader:	*(Holding the large candle high)* Jesus, may your forgiveness be a light for us, that we might forgive one another and create new life in our world.
All:	Amen.

13

Failure: A Time for Faith

Times for Use

Lent, Good Friday, before exams, and any occasion on which failure and loss are topics.

Materials Needed

Newsprint, markers, paper and pencils, and the words "agony of defeat" on a strip of posterboard.

Introduction

One experience that unites human beings is failure. Each of us experiences failure at different times in our lives. The maturity and wisdom each of us gains is a result in some measure of how well we integrate the lessons of failure into our lives.

Our young people need help in understanding the place of failure in their lives. Too often the message they receive is that winning is everything. There is little evidence that they are being given the tools to deal with the failures that are inevitable in life and work, through which they can reach new depths of self-understanding and compassion.

The Scriptures are full of stories about failure and disappointment: Consider the suffering of Job, the righteousness of the prophets over infidelity to the covenant, or the failure of Jesus himself, which resulted in crucifixion. Failure is ever present in the lives of God's people. Faith can help our young people see that their human failures can teach them to depend on God. Through their weakness, they can learn to rely on God's strength.

Shared Experience

Place the words "agony of defeat" in a prominent place in the room. Ask participants to focus on the words and to think of times they have experienced defeat or failure. It need not be something spectacular, but a time when they knew what it felt like to fail.

Next ask them to write down on a piece of paper three ways they have responded to failure. When they fail, experience defeat, or are disappointed, what do they usually do? Invite them to share their responses with one other person.

Getting Started

Leader: We all live in a society that puts great emphasis on winning. Whether playing softball or studying for a test or competing for a job, we are taught to win. We are encouraged to celebrate our successes. But each of us also experiences failure. Who teaches us how to handle failure and to learn from it? Who helps us to grow and mature from facing adversity, rather than to become discouraged and hide? Let us pray over our failures that we may discover a way to face them squarely and to grow through them.

Speaker One: Nice work. I'm sorry you lost. You played well enough to win. Maybe next year. Failed your driving test, that's a shame. Listen it's not your fault, your parents are separating. I know you must feel disappointed. Listen, my friend, you tried your best. It just wasn't good enough.

Speaker Two: All of us has at one time or another experienced a failure and disappointment. We lose games, relationships end, and desired goals are not reached. Times like these can really test our character. The pain is real and deep and seemingly without end. It calls out for a response.

Speaker Three: Some of us may run away from failure by pretending it isn't there. We may cover it with a happy face, a carefree shrug, or false bravery. Others may try to deny or escape the pain of failure through alcohol, drugs, and other diversions.

Speaker Four: But failure can be a great teacher. It can teach us to develop coping skills that are necessary for handling life's problems. Facing our disappointments can help us to know ourselves, our limitations, and our strengths. It can help us to understand the disappointments of others and help them in their moments of sorrow. Such times test our faith in God, the God who knows our pain, stands with us in it, and guides us toward new levels of growth and maturity.

Quiet Time

Reader One: Let's listen to a passage from scripture that describes Jesus

facing the agony of defeat. A reading from Luke (22:39-46):
Then he went out and made his way, as was his custom, to
the Mount of Olives. His disciples accompanied him…

Response
Ask participants to name one way of responding to failure
that shows faith in God. Prayer, talking to a friend, learning
from a mistake, saying "I'm sorry" are some suggestions.
Ask them to write down one suggestion and offer it as gift
to the person next to them.

Conclusion

Leader: Jesus faced his failures and disappointments by handing
                 them over to God, his loving Abba. He did not run away,
                 but in the presence of his friends and with absolute trust in
                 God he admitted his limits and presented them to God.
                 What a wonderful alternative to the very unhealthy ways
                 we often handle our failures. Let's pray together:

Left Side: Lord Jesus, we know that it was for us that you came on
                 earth.

All: Help us to have faith in you.

Right Side: Lord Jesus, we, like you, experience failure.

All: Help us to face our failures and to find friends who will
                 strengthen us in times of disappointment.

Left Side: Lord, let us experience your friendship.

All: Be with us in moments of disappointment, as well as in mo-
                 ments of joy.

Right Side: Lord, let us feel your presence.

All: Be with us in times of failure as well as in times of success.

Leader: Lord Jesus, trusting in your love for us, we ask you to lead
                 us through our failures and disappointments into the joy of
                 new life in your resurrection.

All: Amen.

14

Hope: In the Face of Death

Times for Use
All Soul's Day, Good Friday, and any occasion on which death or loss is the topic.

Materials Needed
A Paschal Candle (or other large candle), six small candles, paper and pencils.

Introduction
Though every moment may be an epiphany of God's presence, there are certain moments that reveal God's presence with particular clarity and transparency. Sometimes these are the brilliance of the ordinary seen through the eyes of faith, but sometimes it is the disruption in our schedules, the unexpected, the painful that brings us to the awareness that we are wrapped in God. Indeed, it is more often when we are forced to question our assumptions about who we are, about the meaning of life that God is revealed.

It could be a long illness, or an accident, the death of a beloved, or even the cruel paradox of experiencing poverty in a world blessed with abundant resources. But in each case we are thrown back on ourselves to cope as best we can with the finality and contingency we might rather ignore each day. At times such as these we are faced with questions and truths that have no easy answers. Our powerlessness in the face of life's trials can lead to faith or despair.

The young, too, should not be denied their right to struggle with life's mysteries that may uncover the possibilities of new life and growth that such struggle can provide. Faith is not meant to take away life's pain but to guide us through it, to elevate our suffering to a new level, revealed in Jesus' paschal mystery.

Shared Experience

Have the room in a soft light. Place one large lit candle, the Paschal Candle if possible, in the front of the room. Place six unlit small candles around the large one. If the group is not too large, have one candle for each person present. Give each person paper and pencil and enough space for a degree of privacy. Ask them to think about their average day and write an outline of it. You may want to verbally outline what you think might be part of an average day. Next, ask them to think of one time when their routine was upset by a painful, unexpected event. Encourage them to write about it including how they felt. You may give an example of this from your own life.

Explain that times of unexpected tragedy can happen to us all. We are going to pray for a greater understanding and acceptance of such moments.

Getting Started

Leader:
Sometimes our daily routines are interrupted by unexpected events. These events can be happy ones, but they may also make us sad. The death of a friend or family member, a classmate in a car accident, or the sudden illness of someone we thought in good health can stop us in our tracks. We may seem dazed. We may feel overcome with sadness, anger, and disbelief. At times such as these we are often filled with questions. We may want to blame someone, God, anyone. We feel powerless and alone. These times can bring us closer to God or we can allow them to separate us from God's love. Let's listen to one person reflect on such a time.

(The following monologue may be read or paraphrased by one of the young people prepared beforehand, or by the leader. You may also break the monologue into parts for different readers.)

Speaker:
I don't understand the accident. It was dark. The road was wet. We were driving too fast. Suddenly there was a crash. When I woke up, I was in the hospital. I didn't find out until the next day that my best friend had died in the crash. Until the time of the accident I was having a pretty ordinary day.

The accident forced me to face the truth that I do not have the control over life I always assumed was mine. Although I can plan and make decisions about my life, there are forces at work in our world I have little or no control over. This realization is troubling me. It can lead me to become cynical at times, thinking life has little meaning. It also helps me appreciate life and my friends and to realize how really precious everything is.

Quiet Time

Reader:

Let us listen together to an event in the life of Jesus that broke his ordinary routine and brought him face to face with the hard realities of life.

A reading from St. Luke (7:11-17): Soon afterward he went to a town called Naim...

(If time permits, you may want to use John's gospel (11:1-44): There was a certain man named Lazarus who was sick... Because of the length of the reading, you may wish to have one person read the narrator's part, one Jesus', and one Martha and Mary's.)

Response

Leader:

We pray that we may experience God's presence in time of pain. It is true we all face moments of shock, moments of intense suffering. We may feel like running away and hiding, but where could we go to leave our pain behind? We also have the opportunity, as Jesus did, to express our suffering in the security of trusted friends, to express our anguish and bring it to God. In faith that God loves us even when we feel most abandoned, in faith that we are loved by compassionate people around us, we can gain the strength and courage to go on.

Conclusion
(Invite one person to come forward to light two of the small candles.)

Left Side:

We are not in total control. Events can happen that cause us deep pain.

All:

Lord, help us to experience your presence in times of sorrow and despair, for you are a faithful God. *(Two more candles are lit.)*

Right Side:

We are not alone. We have each other to be together, to share our anger, to cry with us, and to share our questions.

All:	Lord, give us the courage to be there for each other in times of loneliness and sorrow. *(The remaining candles are lit.)*
Left Side:	Lord, give us hope in Jesus' victory over death. Help us to go to him in time of pain.
All:	Loving God/we are a people formed in faith/in your love for us. In times that seem hopeless,/give us the confidence /to know you are near us./Help us to listen/to each other's questions/to care/and to touch each other's pain./Help us to find hope/in the love of Jesus, your son./Amen. *(An embrace or handshake or a spontaneous sign of care may now be shared.)*

15

Jonah and Jesus: Praying to Our Father

Times for Use
Advent, Epiphany, Lent, as part of confirmation preparation, or on a weekend retreat.

Materials Needed
Pictures of whales, the words of the Our Father on posterboard, paper and pencils.

Introduction
One of the best loved stories in the Hebrew Scriptures is the one about Jonah and the whale. The story instructs us in one of God's greatest gifts, divine mercy. Jonah is a precise reflection of ourselves. Like us, he is afraid of God's compassion and mercy, and resents it when it is bestowed on a people he has decided are unworthy of it. God's embrace of all people regardless of race or nationality and God's unbounded mercy are too much for Jonah—and us—to accept. So he refuses to go to "the foreigners" until, through events beyond his control, he is led to see things from God's perspective.

Jesus' instruction to his disciples on prayer also includes directives on God's mercy available to all. Because we are like Jonah, Jesus makes it clear that only by our forgiveness of others who have harmed us will we become open to God's forgiveness in our own lives. If we hope to become disciples, we are called to relinquish our will to God's will, our limited way of seeing things to God's absolute providence.

Shared Experience
Decorate the room with pictures of whales or one large picture of a whale prominently displayed. You also might have the words to the Our Father in a place of prominence. Ask the young people if they are fa-

miliar with the story of Jonah. If someone is familiar with it, let him or her recount it for the group. If not, you may use the summary below.

Ask the young if they have ever found themselves, like Jonah, going against what they thought or knew was the right thing to do? Can they share one example of what happened in this situation? Have a paper for each person with a whale outlined on it. Ask them to write their names in the center of the whale, along with the names of people or groups of people they have a difficult time accepting. For example, the name John might go in the middle of the whale and the names of rival team members, Asians, and Gary could be around it.

Acknowledge that it is especially hard to be forgiving to a person, group of people, or a nationality that is disliked. We are very much like Jonah in this. This may be one reason Jesus instructs us in the Our Father that we will be forgiven for our failures to the same degree that we forgive one another. Imagine, we are asked to forgive not only those we find it easy to forgive, but also those we find it most difficult to forgive. Only by God's grace, God's activity in our lives, will we do this. We need to pray for this grace.

Jonah was chosen by God to warn the people of Nineveh to change their sinful ways, or calamity would befall them. Jonah did not want to go, since he disliked the Ninevites, and he knew they would repent at his preaching. God's mercy toward all people was too much for poor Jonah. God was too generous! After being thrown overboard in a storm at sea, Jonah spent three days in the belly of a whale. Only then did Jonah change his attitude and preach to the Ninevites, watching them change their ways from evil to repentance.

Getting Started

Speaker One: Sometimes we are like Jonah. There may be a friend or relative or classmate or a person of a certain race who needs God's forgiveness. The only way that person will receive it is through us. Yet, we refuse to assist in this in any way. What God asks is too difficult for us. God is too generous.

Speaker Two: When Jesus taught his followers to pray, he referred to God as a loving father whose mercy is for all people. He also prayed that our sins would be forgiven in the same way we forgive those who wrong us. Let's prepare our hearts now to listen together to God's word.

Quiet Time

Reader One: A reading from Matthew (6:7-15): When you pray, do not behave like the hypocrites...

Response	
Leader:	We will respond to the word of God by bringing the names of people we have difficulty liking to the front and placing them on the table. *(Allow sufficient time for this.)*

Conclusion

Leader: Let us remember Jonah and Jesus and pray that God may offer forgiveness and mercy through our presence to the people we have named.

Left Side: Lord, you are a God of forgiveness and mercy. Help us to be generous in forgiving in order that we may bring your healing presence to our world.

Leader: Let us remember that Jesus became one of us for the benefit of all people. Let us pray for the strength to overcome our prejudices and to extend God's love to all the people we know.

Right Side: Lord, you are the God of all. Help us to be truly catholic. Help us to be open and accepting toward all people, especially those we find it difficult to accept.

All: Help us, loving God, to forgive others as Jesus asks, so that we may experience your forgiveness for our failures. Amen.

16

God Is With Us: In the Flesh

Times for Use
Advent, Christmas, and any occasion on which God's presence is the topic.

Materials Needed
Paints, candles for each participant, pieces of wax, paper and pencils.

Introduction
The mystery of the Incarnation is a celebration of God's love of our humanity. We are so precious that Jesus embraces our human nature that we might return to God as a reborn humanity. But we seem to have a problem accepting the dignity of our being visited by God in this way. The awareness of our sinfulness eclipses our terrible beauty, and the rapture of being human escapes us.

The Incarnation testifies that God came among us with human feet and walked in the mud of human life. This "God among us" depended on the milk from a maiden's breast for sustenance, learned humanity from the example of a simple carpenter, pierced the mystery of life and death and grieved for the dead, embraced children, spent hours in silent prayer, and exhausted himself in the marketplace of human travail. This God knew human love with its moments of play, commitment, and fidelity, and withstood the agony of betrayal. This God of time and eternity is at the center of our human experiences so that we might be at the center of the godhead, sharing God's own life.

Shared Experience
Have the young people decorate candles with paints or

pieces of colored wax. Christmas is a festival of light that celebrates the victory of light and life over the night of darkness and death. The candles can include symbols of hope for the young, names of people who give them hope, or words that spark hope in them.

Ask them to write or mention events of darkness in their lives. Is it family or school or social situations that appear to be dark places for them? Can they also name situations of darkness in our world that are disturbing to them? Is it homelessness, or hunger, or violence, or lack of respect that cause them to worry? Responses may be written out or shared orally. Explain that whatever the worry, Christmas reminds us that God is with us as we struggle to become free and open to lives of love, justice, and generosity.

Getting Started

Leader: Let's reflect together about God becoming one of us in the person of Jesus.

Speaker One: Christmas is coming and it is time to prepare. What does that mean? Buying presents, sending cards, keeping a hectic schedule? People are supposed to be "happy" at Christmas, but we may feel alone or empty if our experience doesn't meet all the expectations. Families are supposed to be happy and celebrate in a loving way together. This is wonderful when it happens, but holidays can also bring out the worst in some families. How are we to celebrate Christmas in a meaningful way?

Speaker Two: Let us begin where we are and try to see our lives in light of the Christmas event. This means recognizing that there is a reality that doesn't depend on our feelings or actions, namely, that God who is beyond time and space entered our world as our friend. We may not always feel God's love because of the lack of love of other people, but Christmas tells us that God is on our side, walking with us through life. We celebrate Jesus' birth in history, aware that he is present now in our lives and with hope in his second coming in glory.

Quiet Time

Reader One: Let us listen to a reading from the gospel of Luke that helps us to realize how God sees us (2:1-26):
In those days a decree went forth...

Response
Have the young people light their candles.

Leader: This is the story of Christmas. This is the story of a God who wants each of us to see ourselves as God sees us. We can look into the eyes of the Christ child, into the eyes of the man Jesus, and discover who we are. We discover that God is not at the fringe of human life but at its very center.

Conclusion

Reader: Loving God, you became one of us to show us our worth.

All: Christ, you are our light.

Reader: Loving God, you became one of us to teach us that love alone will last.

All: Christ, you are our light.

Reader: Loving God, you became one of us to show us how much you love us. Help us to love ourselves and one another with the same love.

All: Christ, you are our light.

Reader: Loving God, you became one of us to show us you are at the center of human life. Help us to pray to you in times of joy and in times of sorrow.

All: Christ, you are our light.

Leader: Lord, you have come to help us overcome the dark places in our lives. May we experience you as our friend who struggles with us in life. Help us to trust that you may be our direction and our light in all of life's unexpected struggles and pain.

All: Amen.

17

Choices: A Path to Freedom

Times for Use

During confirmation preparation, at a weekend retreat, on or near graduation, or any occasion on which decision making is the topic.

Materials Needed

A table and a candle, newsprint, a large question mark drawn on posterboard, small cards for each participant on which are written: "The truth will make you free."

Introduction

Young people today are making choices that can affect them for the rest of their lives. Decisions about sexual activity, dating, staying in school, alcohol and drug use, using violence to resolve conflict, and decisions about their self-worth are some of the many choices being thrust upon them. The media and friends appear to be their main source of advice. How, then, can they make responsible, not to say courageous, decisions?

Shared Experience

Place the large question mark where it can be clearly seen. Invite the young people to spend a few minutes in quiet reflection on the importance of making good decisions. Invite them to share a sample of decisions they have made, and who or what influenced their choices. List some examples on a chart. Ask them to list some of the values that help them to make good decisions, for example, loyalty, honesty, respect, etc.

Getting Started

Leader: We are now going to reflect on the importance of decision making in shaping our lives.

Speaker One:	Life is full of choices. Today some young people are being forced to make some very serious choices. How do you decide? How do you decide about college or career? What guides you in making choices about appropriate sexual behavior on dates? What influences your choice of friends, your decision to drink or to refrain from drinking alcohol? What guides you in your decisions concerning money and possessions, relationships, the poor and suffering?
Speaker Two:	Sometimes we become addicted to those things that promise us freedom: alcohol, popularity, possessions, the need to be right.
Speaker Three:	Isn't it true that sometimes we don't decide? We allow others to determine our choices. Advertisements, TV personalities, and music tell us what to think, what to wear, and how to act. What they are really telling us is what we need to "be" in order to fit into their world.
Speaker Four:	But do we want their values to shape us? Do we want to fit into a world of greed and violence, or do we want to become creators and fashion a new world of our own? The decisions we make today will determine the kind of world we live in tomorrow.

Quiet Time

Leader:	Let's listen to the guidance Jesus offers to help us make good decisions.
Reader:	A reading from John (8:31-31): Jesus then went on to say to those Jews who believed in him: "If you live according to my teaching you are truly my disciples; then you will know the truth and the truth will set you free."
Leader:	Jesus offers no easy answers to the problems and choices that face us. He says if we keep his word in our hearts, we will learn the truth and the truth will set us free. Are we ready for such freedom?

Response

Leader:	Invite the young people to come forward. Hand each in turn a card with these words: "The truth will make you

free." Suggest they take these home and refer to them when they have a hard decision to make.

Conclusion

Side One: Jesus, you don't give easy answers. You invite us to discover who you are by following your way.

All: The truth will make us free.

Side Two: In the struggle to follow your way our eyes will be open to the choices that lead to freedom. Help us never to settle for less.

All: The truth will make us free.

Leader: May the blessing of Jesus be on us; may his word be in our hearts and minds that we may experience true freedom.

All: Amen.

18

Love: A Gift of the Heart

Times for Use

Easter, Pentecost, All Saints Day, Valentine's Day, and on any occasion when unselfish love is the theme.

Materials Needed

Drawings of hearts, pictures of Dorothy Day, Mother Teresa of Calcutta, Archbishop Oscar Romero, Thomas Merton, Nelson Mandela, or Aung San Suu Kyi, newsprint, markers, construction paper, paper and pencils, a poster with these words on it: Decision, Commitment, Knowledge, Consequences, Emotion, Loyalty.

Introduction

One experience stands above all others as a focus of human thought, desire, and activity: the experience of love. Songs are sung about it, plays and poems are written about it. Homilies and sermons are preached about it. People will undergo great difficulties and offer heroic sacrifice, all for love. But the word "love" appears to have lost its power to express the reality. Often the most selfish, petty actions that are contrary to our Christian tradition are described as "love." How can this word regain its rich and clear meaning? The beautiful passage in Corinthians 13, Paul's prayer in Ephesians 3, and the tender lines in the first letter of John are but a sample of the wisdom about love offered in the Scriptures. And who can forget the stirring words of the Song of Solomon or the persistence of the jealous lover in Hosea?

Care, responsibility, knowing the beloved, making an informed decision to love, and experiencing ourselves as loved by God are all part of the reality the Scriptures describe. Divine love took on our flesh in Christ, forever transforming human love.

Shared Experience

Place around the room the drawings of hearts and of people known for their lives of love like Dorothy Day, Mother Teresa, Archbishop Oscar Romero, Aung San Suu Kyi, the winner of the 1991 Nobel Peace Prize, etc. Explain that the theme for this prayer service is love. Ask the young people to draw on construction paper something that is a symbol of love to them. Next ask them to complete the phrase, "Love is...." Invite them to share their responses with the person sitting next to them, or you could write their responses on a chart or chalkboard. Finally, ask them to identify the persons you have pictured for them. Explain why you believe these people are good examples of love.

Getting Started

If possible, have a lectern or reading station with a poster in front of it with these words on it: Decision, Commitment, Knowledge, Consequences, Emotion, Loyalty, etc.

Leader: "I love you with all my heart." These are words we might associate with romantic love or Valentine's Day. "Have you ever said to anyone, 'I love you'?" We begin our prayer service by focusing on love's meaning in our lives.

Speaker One: Is love an emotion that comes and goes and makes us feel warm inside? Or is it a decision to care for another, based on knowledge? Is it a commitment to be responsible for oneself and to be supportive of another in a relationship? Can we truly love someone if we are unable to accept the consequences of our actions?

Speaker Two: This year in our country thousands of young people will become sexually active because they think they are in love. But when feelings change, or someone more interesting comes along, or pregnancy results, this "love" often turns to loneliness, anger, and guilt. Love in these cases is a mask for immaturity.

Speaker Three: When we say we love someone with all our heart, we are affirming that we love from the center of who we are, from the depth of our being. When someone's love is generous, we say she or he is big-hearted. When someone lives fully in the moment, we say that person has "heart."

Speaker Four: Speaking of love and heart, what of Black African Congress

60

leader Nelson Mandela who spent twenty-five years in prison to help bring freedom to the people he loved? Or what of Nobel Peace Prize winner, Aung San Suu Kyi, who has spent over ten years in prison for seeking democracy for the people of Burma she loves? And of course we think of Dorothy Day who opened houses of hospitality for the poor of New York while working and writing tirelessly for peace and nonviolence.

Quiet Time

Reader One: And what of Jesus who said we could have no greater love than to lay down our lives for our friends? Let us spend a few moments listening to what he has to say to us.

A reading from John (15:9-14): As the Father has loved me, so I have loved you. Live on in my love. You will live in my love if you keep my commandments, even as I have kept my Father's commandments, and live in God's love. All this I tell you that my joy may be yours and your joy may be complete. This is my commandment: love one another as I have loved you....You are my friends if you do what I command you. The gospel of the Lord.

Response

Have pieces of paper on a table beside a lit candle. On one side of the paper write beforehand one of the characteristics of love. Examples: Love is a commitment, love takes time, love has consequences. On the other side print the words, "I call you my friend." Ask the young people to come forward to choose a piece of paper. Invite them to pray each day to Jesus, their friend, for help to live out the characteristic of love they have chosen.

Conclusion

Leader: Jesus offers us a great model of love because he did what he said. He knew the joy of loving because he accepted the price demanded by love. We can pray to him to help us to know what love really is.

Left Side: Jesus, help us to know and love ourselves before trying to love another.

Right Side: Jesus, help us to stand by the words we speak and to accept the consequences of our actions.

Left Side: Jesus, you know the price of love. May we reflect on your love and words as we try to live lives of love for each other.

Right Side: Jesus, you decided to love your friends and to accept the consequences of love. Help us to see that love is not achieved by chance but is a conscious decision. Help us to learn to know ourselves and open ourselves to others in honesty and generosity.

All: Loving God/the mystery of your presence/is hidden in nature/in religious symbols/and especially in other persons./ You revealed the true meaning of love in Jesus./ Help us to become passionate lovers like him/so that we may experience the joy of being in union with you/and may your love be made known in us./ Amen.

19

Suffering: A Way to Love

Times for Use
Lent, Holy Week (Good Friday in particular), and any occasion on which suffering is the theme.

Materials Needed
A large cross, paper and pencils.

Introduction
We allow our faith in a just and loving God to be shaken by painful and incomprehensible events, while we often take for granted and think we understand those that bring us joy. An illness or death in the family, financial or emotional losses, the suffering of small children, all challenge our faith. We want someone to be responsible, to feel the loneliness, the powerlessness and anger we feel. But the beauty of a new dawn, the successful completion of another day's work are considered our due.

On careful reflection we see that Jesus reveals a God who heals not only physical ills but also our paralysis of mind and spirit. Jesus uncovers a God who quiets the storms of nature and the storms of the heart. God's word to us in both painful and joyful moments is, "I am with you always, even until the end."

Shared Experience
Place the cross in a prominent place. Ask the young people to take a moment to think about something that has happened to them that was painful, perhaps even something they considered a tragedy. Because of the difficulty in sharing pain, you may want to tell a story of your own, or the following story.

I have a friend who was paralyzed from the neck down in a

boating accident. She was told that she would never live, but through her faith in God and prayer, the support of family and friends, her determination and hard work, and the knowledge and skill of her doctors and nurses, she is now married with a family and can do most things that other people do.

You may give those who are willing, time to share their own stories of pain.

Getting Started

Speaker One: Isn't it amazing! When life stands at our door as a friend, when relationships, school, or work all go well, we take life for granted as if we deserve things to go our way.

Speaker Two: But when life turns its back on us, when tragedy strikes, or we experience disappointment in our relationships, we want to blame God. "Why did God allow it?" we ask. "Why did God take her so young?" "Why me?"

Quiet Time

Reader One: Let us listen to God's word about suffering and faith. A reading from the gospel of Matthew (9:1-8):

Then he re-entered the boat, crossed the lake and came to the other side....

Response

Leader: Ask the young people to think of one person who is suffering. Ask them to think of one thing they could do for the person to show them God's love. These suggestions should be written down and placed on a table in the front of the room.

Conclusion

(Invite participants to stretch out their arms in the fashion of a cross.)

Leader: The door of life opens on both joy and tragedy. The wise person sees the presence of Jesus in all the circumstances of life. His arms are outstretched, full of love and acceptance. He struggles with and shares in our suffering when we are overcome with grief. This is the meaning of love.

(Invite participants to gather in a circle and to hold hands.)

Leader: Loving God, help us to experience your presence in times of hope and in times of despair. Help us not to avoid painful emotions or events. Help us never to blame, but grant us the faith to search out your presence, which is the treasure hidden in the pain.

All: Amen.

20

Prayer: Discipline for Disciples

Times for Use
Lent, Easter, during confirmation preparation, during an extended retreat, or any occasion on which prayer is the topic.

Materials Needed
One large piece of pottery, small pieces of clay, paper and pencils, cards for each participant on which are printed the words: "You are the potter, God; I am the clay."

Introduction
Discipline is a word most of us dislike. It calls to mind some form of bodily punishment, a restraint to freedom, something distasteful and burdensome.

Perhaps the difficulty we have with discipline is that we fail to see it in a positive light. However, it is a good and necessary part of our Christian life. For discipline means to be a disciple. When we are moved by another person or a vision or a great cause, we do what is necessary to take action. We do what we must to follow.

If we think our young people lack discipline, perhaps it is because we don't give them someone to follow. If we want great-hearted young people, we need to introduce them to someone who will challenge them to love. This someone is Jesus. Discipline comes easier when people are reaching out to others with unselfish love in imitation of Jesus.

Shared Experience
Arrange in a prominent place a large piece of pottery and many small pieces of clay. If possible invite a potter to the session to demon-

strate how to work with clay. If this is not possible, invite participants to simply relax and play with the clay. Invite them to feel its consistency, its moistness and texture. When all have created something with the clay, invite those who are willing to describe the experience.

Getting Started

Leader: Ask the young people if they have ever thought of themselves as the clay and God as the potter.

Speaker One: Have you ever watched a potter at work? I have. She sat at her potter's wheel and began to work. She first wet the clay and began to shape it with her slender fingers as it spun on the wheel. I wondered what she would create. It was amazing to watch her remove one piece of the clay, round another, and press yet another piece into the shape she sought. With simple movements marked by grace and ease, she created a delicate vase.

Speaker Two: Lord, you are the potter. With grace and ease you have shaped us into an image of yourself. We, like a piece of pottery, have the mark of our potter within us.

Speaker Three: The potter made it look so easy. I knew I could do it. You can't imagine my frustration and disappointment when my attempts to create something failed. It looked so easy!

Speaker Two: Lord, we forget that those who create beautiful things have spent years disciplining themselves to learn this skill. Whether it's a ballerina or an actor, a baseball player or a singer, those who discipline themselves with hours of practice become free to do what others only dream about. Those who discipline themselves love what they are doing. There is no freedom without discipline, and there is no discipline without love.

Speaker Three: What each of us is creating daily through our decisions to love others is far greater, far more precious than the most spectacular piece of pottery. If we want to be successful in making the pottery of our own life beautiful, we must practice discipline. We need to find something or someone worthy of all our energy and love. When we become disciples of Jesus whom we love, discipline becomes easier.

Reader One: Let's now prepare our hearts and minds to listen to what God said to the prophet Jeremiah about the potter.

Quiet Time

A reading from the book of Jeremiah (18:1-7): This word came to Jeremiah from the Lord: Rise up…

Speaker Four: We are in God's hands. We are the clay into which God has poured life. This is why Jesus so often spent time in prayer and asked his friends to pray. If we are to be disciples of Jesus we need the discipline of prayer. Prayer is the most freeing of all activities. It puts us in touch with God, the source of our life and the one who forms and molds us.

Response
Invite the young people to come forward now to receive the small cards with the quotation, "You are the potter, God; I am the clay," printed on them.

Conclusion
Leader: Lord, it looks easy to create a loving, joyful life, as easy as making a piece of pottery.

All: You are the potter, I am the clay.

Leader: Lord, money, drugs, power, and possessions enslave us and take away our real freedom to create and to love.

All: You are the potter, I am the clay.

Leader: Loving mother and guiding father, help us as we work at the potter's wheel of our own life.

All: You are the potter, I am the clay.

Leader: May God, our loving potter, bless each of you in the name of the Father, Son, and Holy Spirit.

All: Amen.

Of Related Interest...

Weekly Prayer Services for Teenagers
Lectionary-Based for the School Year (Years A and B)
M. Valerie Schneider, S.N.D.
These 37 prayer services are intended for junior and senior high school students, both in Catholic school and religious education settings. These services involve teenagers in a dramatic reading of Scripture, include questions for reflection and discussion, a time for communal prayer, and an activity. Themes cover generosity, forgiveness, sacrifice, discipleship, holiness, academics, baptismal commitment, liturgical seasons, and more.

ISBN: 0-89622-692-1, 104 pp, $12.95 (order M-72)

Also available in Years B & C—ISBN: 0-89622-732-4, 112 pp, $12.95 (order B-34)

Confirmed in the Spirit
Prayer Services for Confirmation Classes and Retreats
M. Valerie Schneider, S.N.D.
The author believes that preparing high school students for confirmation should be a way of preparing them for life. Through ritual actions, Scripture readings, group prayers and reflections, these 20 prayer services help place the sacrament in a broader context and remind students that their commitment involves a lifelong responsibility. Includes 35 brief prayers for beginning or ending class and suggestions for additional activities. Perfect for teachers, catechists, pastors, DREs, youth ministers, sponsors, and parents too!

ISBN: 0-89622-655-7, 88 pp, $12.95 (order M-43)

Seasonal Prayer Services for Teenagers
Greg Dues
This collection of 16 prayer services helps teenagers understand the themes found in seasonal, church, and civic holidays. From Autumn to Advent to May, teens will find these services lively, thoughtful, and deeply involving.

ISBN: 0-89622-473-2, 80 pp, $9.95 (order C-53)

Teenagers Come and Pray!
Celebrating Milestones, Memorials, and Holy Days
Michael D. Ausperk
Here are 26 practical and pertinent prayer services for use throughout the school year which help modern teenagers find a sense of their own spirituality and responsibility as Christians amid the other demands in their lives. Topics covered include: beginning the school year, before a performance or competition, respect for life, on the death of a classmate or teacher, confirmation, and recovering from an addiction. This is the ideal book for catechists, youth ministers, religion teachers, and anyone struggling with the question of how to make religion more relevant to teenagers today.

ISBN: 0-89622-642-5, 112 pp, $12.95 (order M-35)

20 More Teen Prayer Services
Kevin Regan
Each prayer service contains a mini-lesson, and includes suggested times for use, a list of materials needed, an introduction, shared experience, and the prayer service. Topics cover peer pressure, athletics, violence, drug abuse, self-image, and more.

ISBN: 0-89622-605-0, 112 p, $9.95 (order M-04)

Available at religious bookstores or from:

TWENTY-THIRD PUBLICATIONS
P.O. Box 180 • Mystic, CT 06355

For a complete list of quality books and videos call:
1 - 8 0 0 - 3 2 1 - 0 4 1 1